Compost Center Operator

Published in the United States of America by The Child's World®
1980 Lookout Drive • Mankato, MN 56003-1705
800-599-READ • www.childsworld.com

Acknowledgments
The Child's World®: Mary Berendes, Publishing Director
Red Line Editorial: Editorial direction
The Design Lab: Design
Amnet: Production

Photographs ©: Kevin Clark/AP Images, cover; Jeff Gynane/
Thinkstock, 5; Meg Wallace Photography/Shutterstock Images,
7; Environmental Protection Agency, 9; Nikolay100/Thinkstock,
11; Rikard Stadler/Shutterstock Images, 13; Tony Avelar/
AP Images, 15; Huguette Roe/Shutterstock Images, 16; Axel
Heimken/AP Images, 19; Waverly Wyld/Thinkstock, 20

ISBN 9781631436857
LCCN 2014945298

Printed in the United States of America
Mankato, MN
November, 2014
PA02238

ABOUT THE AUTHOR

Mirella S. Miller is an author and editor living in Minnesota. She once helped her dad build a backyard compost pile. One day, she hopes to have her own backyard compost pile.

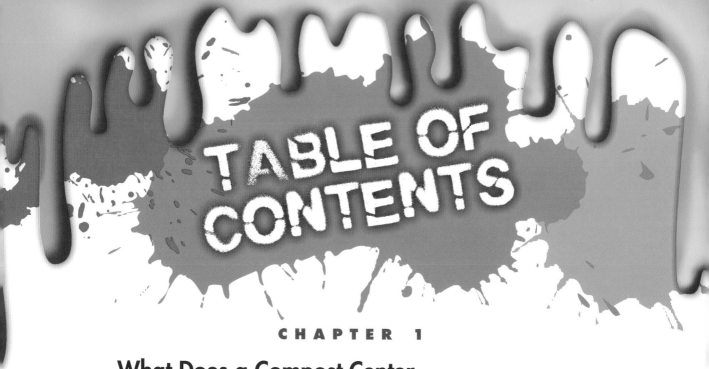

TABLE OF CONTENTS

CHAPTER 1

What Does a Compost Center Operator Do?

Humans produce a lot of trash. It ends up in landfills. Landfills hurt the environment. But not everything that ends up in a landfill needs to be there. Many people recycle their plastic, metal, and paper. But not as many recycle their **organic** matter. Organic matter includes food scraps and yard waste. These things naturally **decompose**. But people can speed up the process. This is called composting. Waste that is composted does not end up in landfills. Compost is used in gardens. It improves the soil.

Some people compost in their backyards. Others even compost in tiny apartments! But not everyone has enough time or space to take care of compost piles. These people rely on compost centers. These facilities take in a lot waste.

Backyard compost
bins can be made
of wood, plastic, or
even chicken wire.

They make a lot of compost. Compost center operators make the facilities run smoothly. They make the compost. Then they sell the finished product. Customers use the compost on their gardens. It helps their plants grow better.

Compost is made up of greens and browns. Greens are grass clippings and food scraps. Dry leaves, mulch, and branches are browns. Compost center operators make sure there is the right amount of greens and browns in the mixture. Too much of one or the other slows down the composting. It can also make the compost smell.

DISGUSTING!

If there are too many greens in compost or not enough oxygen, it smells like rotten eggs. Compost operators fix it by adding more browns. They also turn the pile. This makes the pile smell less bad.

Bacteria and other **microorganisms** eat the greens and browns. They change them into compost. People can create conditions that help

Food scraps can be put in a backyard compost bin (pictured) or brought to a compost center.

bacteria do their work. People make sure the temperature is right. They make sure the bacteria have enough water and air. The bacteria thrive in these conditions. They eat faster than they would naturally. Decomposition happens much more quickly than in the wild if the conditions are right. The mixture of greens and browns begins to transform. In a few months it will be compost.

CHAPTER 2

A Day on the Job

Trash trucks collect food waste and yard waste from some homes and businesses. Then they take it to the compost center. People also drop off their own waste. The compost center operator drives a **front-end loader**. The machine scoops up the greens and browns. It carries the waste to a mixing area.

Workers must remove non-compostables from the waste. These include plastic and glass. In some centers, the waste moves on conveyer belts past workers. The workers use their hands to remove things from the waste that shouldn't be there. Sorting through waste by hand is gross and dangerous. Workers must wear gloves and safety glasses. This protects them against cuts and disease. In other centers a machine does the sorting.

A sign posted in a compost center shows items that can be composted in that facility.

Now the waste is free of non-compostables. A machine mixes the greens with the browns. It adds the right amount of each. This will help the matter decompose correctly. The completed mixture is moved to another area of the center for composting.

Operators shape the waste into long piles called **windrows**. As the bacteria eat, they give off heat. The piles heat up. Workers must carefully monitor the temperature. If it gets too hot or too cold, the bacteria slow down. They could even die. Workers use a big thermometer. The compost should be heating up to at least 131 degrees Fahrenheit (55°C). That is almost as warm as the highest surface temperature ever recorded on Earth!

DISGUSTING!
Flies lay eggs in a compost pile. Maggots hatch from the eggs. Then the maggots eat the waste.

If the temperature is too high, the pile may begin to burn. This can be unsafe for workers. If a pile gets warmer than 170 degrees Fahrenheit (77°C), an operator needs to turn

A compost pile gives off steam as it heats up.

the pile. The worker uses a front-end loader. The machine moves material from the outside to the inside of the pile. This "fluffs" the material. More air gets in. Decomposition speeds up.

Operators can control how much air blows through the compost. Bacteria need oxygen to do their work. Workers keep the air flowing. The bacteria eat faster.

After eight to ten months the bacteria slow down. The piles begin to cool. Workers use the front-end loader to move the compost to a curing area. They stack the compost in big piles. The compost stays in a curing pile until it is finished. During this time, workers turn the pile. This helps air move through. The pile cools down.

Looking at a compost pile helps an operator know when it is finished. The compost is ready when no large pieces of food or yard waste can be seen. It should look like soil. Compost is dark, crumbly, and uniform in texture. The pile should not look like

TECHNOLOGY

Compost centers use a lot of big equipment. A screener removes things from the compost that should not be there anymore. These include plastic bottles or wrappers. Old screeners did not always catch these bottles. New screeners shake the matter onto different levels. These machines move compost much faster than old machines. This means compost centers can keep more waste out of landfills each year.

Front-end loader

Screener

A front-end loader empties compost into a screener.

it did when it was first mixed. Finished compost will not be warm anymore. It will have an earthy smell. The compost can be moved to a screener. This machine removes any large pieces that were missed earlier. Now the compost is ready to be sold.

CHAPTER 3

Why Composting Matters

Composting has been around for a long time. Ancient peoples may have used compost for farming. They would have seen that putting compost on their soil helped crops grow. But they didn't know how compost worked.

In the early 1900s, a British scientist named Sir Albert Howard began testing compost mixtures. He wanted to find the best one. He wrote a book about his work. U.S. farmers used this information to improve their soil.

TECHNOLOGY

Sir Albert Howard spent 30 years studying farming. He wanted to improve farmers' crops. His best compost had three parts plant matter and one part manure. Howard layered the matter. It also helped to add a layer of soil and a layer of rock. If the pile was kept wet, the compost could be ready in three months. Compost centers continue to improve the compost recipe today.

Trucks spread compost on fields to help crops grow.

Farmers and gardeners around the world continue to compost. Adding compost to soil helps plants and crops grow. It also keeps soil healthy. Healthy soil leads to healthy plants and animals.

Composting helps
keep waste out
of landfills.

More than 60 percent of compostable matter ends up in landfills today. Many people compost to create less waste. They keep a compost pile at their home or farm. The average U.S. household creates more than 650 pounds (295 kg) of compostable waste each year!

As of 2012, more than 150 communities in the United States had programs to collect food waste from homes. As these programs expand, there will be a greater need for compost center operators. Compost operators turn this waste into a usable product. Bringing compostable waste to a compost center helps the environment.

DISGUSTING!

Vermicomposting uses worms to turn food waste into healthy soil. The worms' job is to eat waste. They turn the waste into worm droppings. Worm droppings contain nutrients that make soil healthier. Vermicomposting is used in big centers and in backyard bins.

CHAPTER 4

Overcoming Problems

Operators have to check on the compost piles often. There is a lot that can go wrong. Piles can get too hot or too cold. Checking the temperature and turning compost piles can be gross. Workers get decomposed food scraps on their clothes. Sometimes compost piles smell. A smelly pile is a sign that something is wrong. Operators must fix this problem quickly. Adding water or turning the pile may solve the problem.

Workers use big and dangerous machines. They must dress for safety. They wear a hard hat, safety glasses, and steel-toed boots. A reflective shirt, jacket, or vest is also part of the uniform. This helps workers see each other at all times so that they don't hurt each other with the heavy equipment. If a piece of equipment is not working properly, an operator must stop working. Compost centers make sure workers are not hurt by broken machines.

A worker at a
compost facility in
Germany operates
a machine.

It is important to know what can and cannot go in a compost bin.

Compost centers attract animals that want to feed on the food waste. Workers must keep animals away while staying safe. All kinds of animals try to get into compost centers. Rodents, coyotes, and raccoons are a few examples. Operators must always be on the lookout and keep animals away.

Most people are unfamiliar with the dos and don'ts of composting. This is one of the biggest problems operators face. This means people put the wrong things in compost bags. Dairy and meat products cannot be composted. Glass and tin also are not compostable. Workers spend lots of time sorting through food waste. Waste with sharp edges can cut a worker. But you can help! Learn what can and cannot be composted. Teach your classmates and your relatives. Start a backyard compost pile of your own!

Composting can be a gross job. But workers turn waste into healthy soil. They work hard to recycle naturally.

GLOSSARY

decompose (dee-kuhm-POZE) To decompose is to slowly break down naturally. Mixing compost correctly helps it decompose more quickly.

front-end loader (FRUNT END LOHD-ur) A front-end loader is a machine like a tractor with a big bucket or shovel attached to the front. A compost center operator uses a front-end loader to turn compost piles and to move matter around.

microorganisms (mye-kroh-OR-guh-niz-uhmz) Microorganisms are living things so small they cannot be seen with the naked eye. Microorganisms live in dirt, food, and even the human body.

organic (or-GAN-ik) Things that are organic come from living things. Operators mix organic matter together.

windrows (WIN-drohz) Windrows are long rows of compost heaped together. Compost operators must tend the windrows carefully.

TO LEARN MORE

BOOKS

Davies, Stephanie. *Composting Inside & Out*. Ontario, Canada: Betterway Home Books, 2011.

Siddals, Mary McKenna. *Compost Stew: An A to Z Recipe for the Earth*. New York: Crown Publishing Group, 2010.

Strauss, Rachelle. *Compost: How to Use, How to Make, Everyday Tips*. London: Flame Tree Publishing Company, 2009.

WEB SITES

Visit our Web site for links about compost center operators: *childsworld.com/links*

Note to Parents, Teachers, and Librarians: We routinely verify our Web links to make sure they are safe and active sites. So encourage your readers to check them out!

INDEX